HOW TO PLAN YOUR COMPETITIVE STRATEGY

HOW TO PLAN YOUR COMPETITIVE STRATEGY

Enjoy the benefits of good planning

Sarah Layton, Alfred Hurd and William Lipsey

KOGAN PAGE

Copyright © Crisp Publications Inc 1995

All rights reserved. No part of this book may be reproduced or transmitted in any form or by any means now known or to be invented, electronic or mechanical, including photocopying, recording, or by any information storage or retrieval system, without written permission from the author or publisher, except for the brief inclusion of quotations in a review.

First published in the United States of America in 1995, entitled *Competitive Strategy*, by Crisp Publications Inc, 1200 Hamilton Court, Menlo Park, California 94025, USA.

This edition first published in Great Britain in 1996 by Kogan Page Ltd, 120 Pentonville Road, London N1 9JN.

British Library Cataloguing in Publication Data

A CIP record for this book is available from the British Library.

ISBN 0-7494-1907-5

Typeset by BookEns Ltd, Royston, Herts.
Printed and bound in Great Britain by Clays Ltd, St Ives plc.

Contents

About This Book 7

Introduction 9

Planning: The Key to Competitive Strategy 11
    Starting out *11*
    Benefits *15*

Step 1. Preplanning 19
    Finding a director *19*
    Finding a coordinator *21*
    Choosing team members *21*
    Director meets the chief executive *22*
    Director meets individual team members *25*
    Team tasks and data-gathering worksheets *25*

Step 2. Intelligence Gathering 45
    Gathering information *45*
    Where to find information *47*

Step 3. Analysis 50
    The two-level approach *50*

Step 4. Building the Plan 58
    Preparing for the planning session *58*
    The planning session *59*
    The sum of all action plans *73*

Step 5. Implementation   79
    Managing projects   79
    The ten essentials of project planning   82

Step 6. Control and Follow-Up   87
    Project control   87
    Goals   89
    Summary   90

About This Book

How to Plan Your Competitive Strategy is not like most books. It has a unique self-paced format that encourages a reader to become personally involved. Designed to be read with a pencil, there are exercises, activities, assessments and cases that invite participation.

This book focuses on competitive strategy planning, a team-based process that helps organisations to build a competitive advantage in the marketplace by developing and implementing strategies that grow the business.

How to Plan Your Competitive Strategy can be used effectively in a number of ways. Here are some possibilities:

- **Individual study.** Because the book is self-instructional, all that is needed is a quiet place, some time and a pencil. Completing the activities and exercises will provide valuable feedback, as well as practical ideas for improving your business successes and profitability.
- **Workshops and seminars.** This book is ideal for use during, or as pre-assigned reading prior to, a workshop or seminar. With the basics in hand, the quality of participation will improve. More time can be spent practising concept extensions and applications during the programme.

There are other possibilities that depend on the objectives of the user. One thing is certain: even after it has been read, this book will serve as excellent reference material that can be easily referred to again.

Introduction

How to Plan Your Competitive Strategy presents a well-tested process for bringing the future into the present so a management team can act *now* to shape the future. That team may come from any organisation: businesses, non-profit organisations, volunteer groups, churches, even families. Whenever people are gathered for mutual benefit, they can profit from planning their competitive strategy.

Although one new initiative after another (such as Total Quality Management – or TQM – Rightsizing, Downsizing, Empowerment, and the like) has swept through corporate life, strategic planning for competitive advantage remains fundamental to all these management tools.

A survey of over 200 executives in North America reported in *Management Review*[1] found that 42 per cent had adopted 11 or more initiatives within the preceding five years and 60 per cent reported three or more initiatives in the last year and a half. Although two-thirds reported short-term gains, a full two out of three admitted that their internal structures and employee morale were 'worse' or 'the same'! All these initiatives can be valuable when they are applied to achieve the vision of an organisation's competitive strategy – but these tools are seldom ends in themselves.

This book uses business examples to illustrate the competitive strategy process, but the reader can easily

---

1. *Management Review*, The American Management Association, October 1994.

translate business titles and areas of interest to their own organisation; for example, 'Head of Finance' can be understood as 'Treasurer' and 'Gross Revenue' as 'Grants' or 'Contributions'.

Readers who want to develop a competitive strategy for their own organisations can use this book as their guide. It describes the process of developing a competitive strategy; readers use their experience with their own particular business to generate the insights and creativity needed to understand issues, solve problems, and set new directions. The team that follows the process presented in this book – working through all its parts and thoughtfully completing all exercises – will produce a rewarding competitive strategy. In addition, they will find themselves more than ever united as an effective team, and they will have learned much about how to manage the projects and the managers that will implement the plan. After all, research shows that organisations with a sound competitive strategy and effective implementation have a bottom-line growth of 10 per cent per year compared with only 1 per cent for organisations without such a strategy.[2]

---

2. Based on research conducted in 1991 by Mishalanie, Layton & Associates, Inc.

Planning: The Key to Competitive Strategy

Starting out

How to Plan Your Competitive Strategy answers the question: 'How do we get where we want to go with what we have or can get?' Successful answers are based on a great deal of straightforward hard work illuminated by creativity at critical points. It is easy to understand but difficult to do. It is difficult because creating an effective competitive strategy requires senior managers to take time from their daily routine and think strategically and hard about their business, their competition, the marketplace and the environment. This kind of thinking and the data gathering it requires are often unfamiliar, but senior managers are responsible for strategy. This book tells them how to do the work that leads to competitive success.

The core process in developing a competitive strategy for your organisation or for yourself is planning. Generally speaking, competitive strategy planning concentrates on new directions and growth more than on cost savings and efficiencies of operation. It concentrates on top line rather than bottom line improvement. Both elements are addressed, of course, but the outward-looking view of competitive strategy towards customers and markets takes precedence.

It is also important to understand what the process is *not*. It is not a long-term financial projection, nor is it individual managers filling out a preordained set of forms. It is not next year's budget or operating plan. Rather, competitive strategy planning is a team-based process that focuses on building competitive advantage in the marketplace by developing and implementing strategies that build the business. It absolutely requires the involvement of senior management for its development and the whole organisation's commitment to its implementation. Without these, any plan is a worthless document no matter how handsomely produced and bound.

Simply stated, the process of developing a competitive strategy asks and answers three questions:

- Where are we?
- Where do we want to be?
- How can we get there?

Once the competitive strategy is clear, implementation can follow, secure in the knowledge that the chosen tasks are the best and wisest for the organisation.

A six-part process

The process of developing a competitive strategy has six parts, each of which differs sharply from the others. Every one is vital and the six must be done strictly in sequence. The diagram *Competitive Strategy Development Process* on page 14 illustrates these steps, and the chapters that follow discuss them in detail:

1. **Preplanning**
   Selecting and training the team and organising for planning.

2. **Intelligence gathering**
   Collecting data about products, markets, government regulations and technology, as well as about competitors, customers and employees for every aspect of your business.

3. **Analysis**
   Thinking about what the data mean and using this meaning to illuminate management's understanding of the business.

4. **Building the plan**
   Using the results of the team's analysis to go from the general to the specific by confirming directions and establishing goals as springboards for designing effective strategies and tactics and setting measurements for success.

5. **Implementation**
   Undertaking projects (usually) outside routine administrative assignments.

6. **Control and follow-up**
   Keeping regular track of progress and modifying plans as appropriate both to establish how far you have come and as a basis for next year's planning.

The benefits of thoughtful planning are set out on page 15.

How to Plan Your Competitive Strategy

Competitive Strategy Development Process

How to get where you want to go with what you have or can get

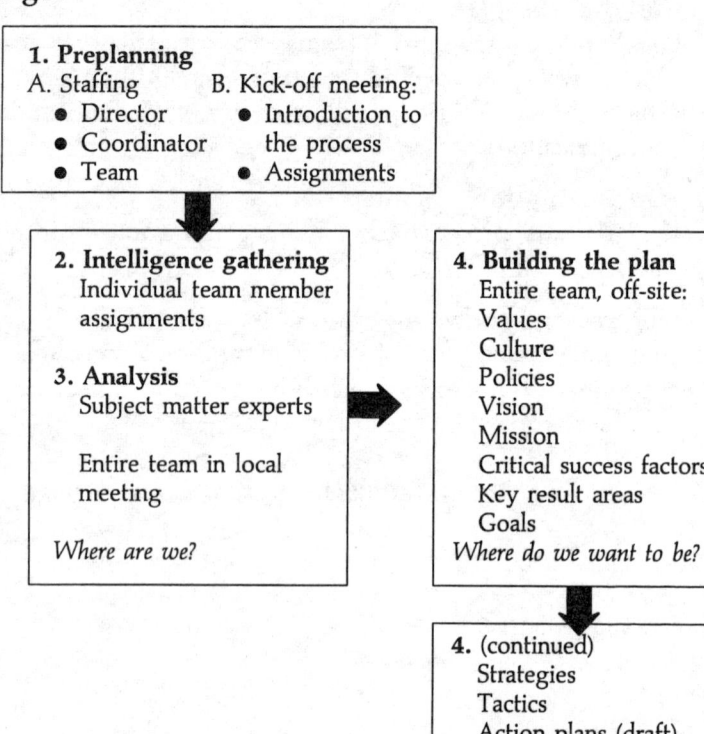

1. Preplanning
A. Staffing
- Director
- Coordinator
- Team

B. Kick-off meeting:
- Introduction to the process
- Assignments

2. Intelligence gathering
Individual team member assignments

3. Analysis
Subject matter experts

Entire team in local meeting

Where are we?

4. Building the plan
Entire team, off-site:
Values
Culture
Policies
Vision
Mission
Critical success factors
Key result areas
Goals

Where do we want to be?

4. (continued)
Strategies
Tactics
Action plans (draft)
Controls
Sharing the vision

Entire team, local meeting:
Action plans (final)
Sum of all action plans

How can we get there?

5. Implementation

6. Control and follow-up

Benefits

The benefits of thoughtful planning fall into four groups:

1. **Financial results**
   Many organisations have found that planning increases revenues or market share or both; some find that planning is the way to save their failing business.
2. **Team building**
   Real team building takes place when a group works hard on important matters; few tasks are more critical to an organisation than competitive strategy planning, and the people who develop these strategies come to trust and depend on one another in ways that serve the organisation from then on.
3. **Organisational strength**
   Senior managers often say, after working through the process, that they understand their organisation better than ever – sometimes in new ways. Additional benefits are that participants in the process develop as managers by learning to think strategically, and new managers on the team quickly learn about the company in great detail.
4. **Business reality**
   Because the planning team analyses the implications of a variety of information and because many habitual ways of operating are examined critically (often for the first time), the team has a fresh and clear-sighted understanding of exactly how the business stands in relation to the outside world and what strengths and problems the company possesses. Often prejudices about fellow team members dissolve as everyone contributes their best; sometimes, unqualified managers are unmasked.

Process timeline
The lines on the *Suggested Planning Schedule* shown overleaf represent elapsed calendar time for a typical strategy planning process through its various parts. The values it contains are averages based on experience with hundreds of organisations

How to Plan Your Competitive Strategy

and will give you a sense of how long your process might take and, especially, what proportion of the time will most likely be spent on each part.

Suggested Planning Schedule

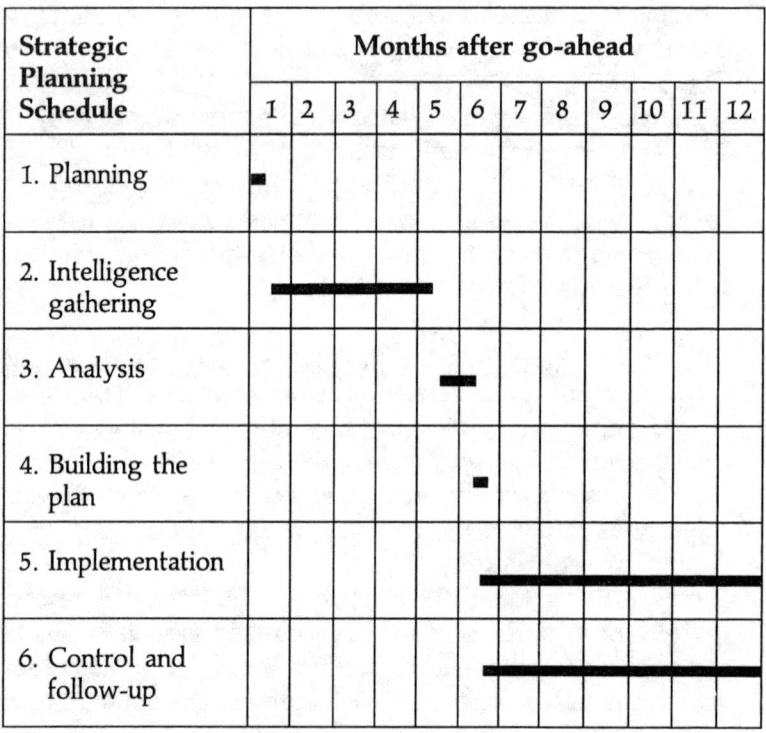

Strategic Planning Schedule	Months after go-ahead												
	1	2	3	4	5	6	7	8	9	10	11	12
1. Planning												
2. Intelligence gathering												
3. Analysis												
4. Building the plan												
5. Implementation												
6. Control and follow-up												

Reprinted with permission of Dr Sarah Layton.

Some questions as you approach competitive strategy planning

Ask yourself or your team these questions to begin the process of framing a realistic and effective competitive strategy. The easier the answers come, the more ready you are to plan effectively.

Planning: The Key to Competitive Strategy

1. Who in your company is involved in thinking about the future?

   _____
   _____
   _____
   _____

2. How do you keep track of your competition?

   _____
   _____
   _____
   _____

3. Where do you believe your market is going?

   _____
   _____
   _____
   _____

4. Why is your company successful or why is it not?

   _____
   _____
   _____
   _____

5. How is strategy developed in your company?

   _____
   _____
   _____
   _____

6. How does your business compare with projections from a year ago?

___

7. What level of teamwork exists in your top management group?

___

8. What kinds of problem do you find in implementing strategy?

___

Step 1
Preplanning

Finding a director

In the same way that planning your competitive strategy is crucial to success, planning to develop your strategic plan is equally important. This section of the book deals with planning to plan.

There are two parts to every piece of work: *what* you are doing and *how* you are doing it. Experience shows that the best plans are made when the team concentrates on the 'what' and a director concentrates on the 'how'. The person selected for this vital role must be capable in four areas:

- They must know the planning process.
- They must be skilful facilitators.
- The should be unbiased outsiders.
- They must have broad business knowledge and experience with many organisations.

All this enables the director to ask shrewd questions and help the team to synthesise the volumes of intelligence that will be developed.

Knowledge of process means that this person must know the steps of plan building thoroughly and can keep track of the team's progress. Also, this person should be able to extend or abbreviate parts of the process wisely – depending on what is most important to the team, while still completing every step of the process and finishing the plan on schedule. This allows team members to remain in their management roles.

Often, a team fails to challenge one another's assumptions by asking unsettling questions. It is the director's job to challenge sacred cows, uncritical assumptions and foggy thinking. Typically, the team learns from the director's behaviour to ask difficult but important questions. This willingness to ask such questions is a critical lesson for planning-team members.

Case study

> **Learning from competitors**
> Often, an organisation's pride leads it to be scornful of competitors. One successful software company, analysing a major competitor, decided that the competitor's long-term chance of success was small because their software architecture was inferior. Nevertheless, the competitor appeared successful. Probing questions by the planning director elicited the information that although the competitor's products might be technically inferior, they had 'user friendliness' that appealed to customers. This insight caused the planning team to reassess the competitor and, ultimately, develop a strategy that focused equally on user friendliness and product technology.

To fulfil this role, the director with broad business experience does *not* need much experience with the business of your particular company. The detachment of a shrewd outside business generalist is a valuable ingredient in the planning process.

A skilled outsider is the most effective choice for director. But sometimes a small organisation cannot afford outside help and decides to use one of their own members as directors. This can work if the company chooses a tough-minded person who understands the need to shift back and forth between emphasising 'what' is being done versus 'how' it is being accomplished. Look for someone with experience facilitating other kinds of processes, such as problem solving, who will also learn the planning process thoroughly and has a general business outlook. When an internal director is used, it is vital to the planning process (and the director's career) that the whole team — especially the chief executive — allow that person to perform his or her assigned role fully without fear of recrimination for asking probing questions.

Finding a coordinator

The coordinator administers the planning project by seeing that work assignments are done on schedule and that everything is ready for the off-site planning session including transport, transparencies, notebooks, and the like. Afterwards, the coordinator administers the implementation phase since the plan's success depends on persistent follow-up and attention to detail. A director who is a member of the organisation might also do this job. But the talents needed to direct a planning session differ from those needed to keep track of tasks and make arrangements; not everyone can do both well. Most organisations will be best served by assigning these two roles to different people; the chief executive should not undertake either one.

Choosing team members

The planning team should always include the senior officers of the organisation — those who report directly to the chief executive. After all, it is their job to set the company's strategic direction. The team should also include those responsible for key operational areas if they are not part of the senior management group in your organisation. For example, if the heads of information systems or human resources are outside that group, consider the value of including them.

Remember: When the planning process is complete, each

team member must meet specific measurable goals that support the company's competitive strategy. Choose people with the knowledge, resources and the will to discharge their responsibilities successfully throughout the strategic planning process and afterwards. Everyone must be an effective participant.

The larger the team, the longer team meetings will take. Each person is there to contribute and deserves time to be heard. There should be no observers.

Director meets the chief executive

As the first step in the planning process, the director meets the chief executive to discuss several important items. The first is the reason for conducting a planning session at this time. Reasons range from imminent bankruptcy or uncontrolled growth to the simple sense that the company ought to be doing better. Each suggests different goals and process emphasis.

The director must know the chief executive's attitude towards planning. Planning is most effective when the chief executive is prepared to rely on the senior management group and endorse new directions based on their collective thinking.

The two should discuss what the planning process is to accomplish in broad terms. The general target might be a strategy for survival, growth or profitability, for increasing market share, or even for selling the company itself. The specifics of these goals, such as actual percentages, come later after analysis at plan-building time.

They should establish the history and results of any previous company planning – what strategic planning has been done and whether or not it was successful. The director is interested in whatever positive or negative expectations the team will bring into the strategic planning process. For example, a poor experience may have left them suspicious or discouraged, or a partial effort may have given them a head start on intelligence gathering.

Another topic is the composition of the planning team, the

Preplanning

special contributions to be expected from each, and the relationships among them. The director and chief executive need to assign work groups and leaders based on individual talent and experience. Also, it is useful for the director to have the chief executive's perceptions about the dynamics of the management team — partly to keep the process smooth and partly to compare what really happens with the chief executive's expectations.

The director and chief executive should establish the planning schedule from the preplanning meeting through to the start of implementation.

The team meeting

Every project starts with a kick-off meeting when the chief executive introduces team members to the goals of the project, their roles and responsibilities, how the work will be organised and what the rewards or penalties may be. In addition, the director must explain the planning process and train individuals in intelligence gathering and strategic thinking.

This meeting takes about half a day during which the director tells the team about the planning process and their parts in it. The topics that must be covered are presented in brief here; the chapters that follow give specifics.

- The president or chief executive begins the meeting by endorsing the importance of developing a competitive strategy for the company and noting that the team here assembled has been carefully chosen to do this vital work — no one else is determining the future of the company.
- The director describes the process of developing a competitive strategy from preplanning through to control and follow-up using the pyramid shown here to illustrate how each part builds on previous parts.

How to Plan Your Competitive Strategy

Competitive Strategy Team Planning Process

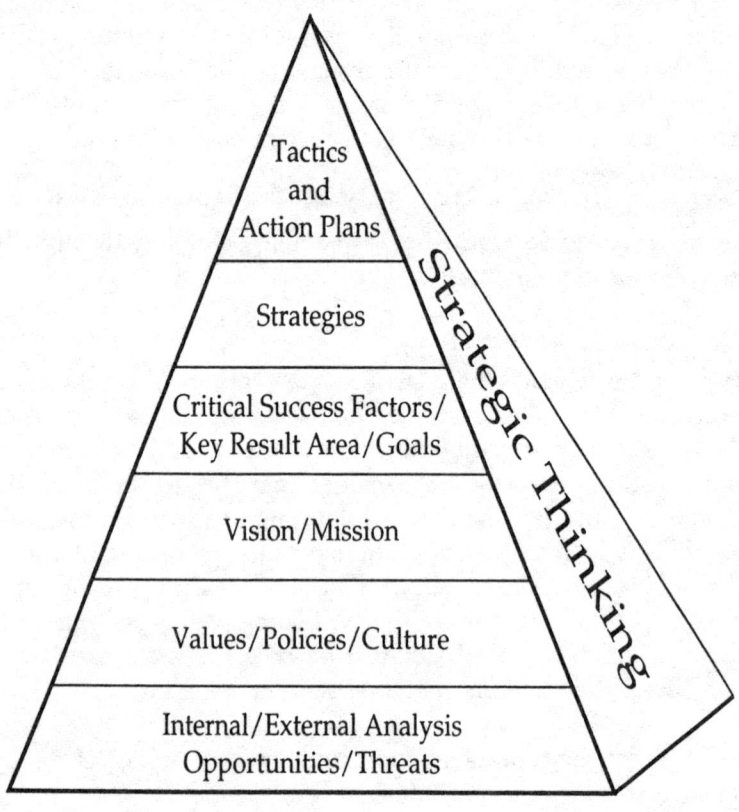

Reprinted by permission of the Hamilton Strategic Management Group.
© Hamilton Strategic Management Group, 1994.

- The director next assigns intelligence gathering to the appropriate people by handing out and discussing the forms provided in Step 2, Intelligence Gathering. These forms address areas such as the company's financial situation and history, the market, products and services, employees, customers, competition and corporate culture. Note that the forms provided may not exactly fit your organisation. Feel free to modify them to make them more useful.

- The director then discusses strategic thinking by noting that every team member must play two roles: as a subject matter expert and as a senior manager concerned with the company as a whole. Success demands that typical departmental rivalries be minimised for the good of the enterprise as a whole.

Director meets individual team members

After the meeting, the director meets each team member individually to discuss candidly each of their expectations for, and reservations about, the process. Typically, in this discussion, the director addresses unrealistic hopes and fears by describing the experience of other planning teams and clarifies misunderstandings about the tasks of the planning process.

Also, the director makes sure that all team members understand their intelligence-gathering assignments and have the time and resources along with a rough plan for accomplishing the work.

Team tasks and data-gathering worksheets

The worksheets are listed below. Each worksheet has directions for data gathering.

Director
  Planning Organisation Worksheet   Form 1 (page 28)

Chief Executive
  Environmental Analysis   Form 2 (page 29)
  Current Corporate Organisation   Form 3 (page 30)

Head of Finance
  Financial Analysis:
    Profit and Loss Summary (000)   Form 4 (page 32)
    Profit and Loss Summary
      (% of Net Sales)   Form 5 (page 33)

Balance Sheet Summary (000)   Forms 6A and 6B
[Assets/Liabilities and Net Worth]   (pages 34 and 35)
Selected Financial Ratios   Form 7 (page 36)
Personnel Data   Form 8 (page 37)
Financial History and Current Situation:

The head of finance also prepares a summary of the company's financial history and current situation (from the present back three to five years) for presentation at the opening of the strategic planning session. As appropriate, this presentation illustrates key elements from these worksheets with graphs or charts.

Head of Marketing

Marketing Analysis:
Sales Mix   Form 9 (page 38)
For each market segment and competitor:
Market Segment Profile   Form 10 (page 39)
Competitor Strengths and Weaknesses   Form 11 (page 40)

Human Resources Manager

Employee Survey (if available) on job satisfaction, management, ideas for improving operations, training and other job needs

All Team Members

General Organisation Data
(In their areas of responsibility)   Form 12 (page 41)
Corporate Climate Assessment   Form 13 (pages 42–44)

Preplanning Guideline

Following the team meeting, participants should be able to articulate goals, timetable, responsibilities and expectations. The items given here can serve as your guideline.

Team Meeting Summary

- Corporate planning goals: _____

_____

_____

- Planning schedule: _____

_____

_____

- My roles and responsibilities: _____

_____

_____

- My data-gathering areas: _____

_____

_____

- My expectations for the planning process: _____

_____

_____

How to Plan Your Competitive Strategy

Planning Organisation Worksheet   Form 1

Team member name and title	Address and telephone/ fax numbers
Director: Coordinator: Team members:	

Preplanning

Environmental Analysis Form 2

List here the key factors external to your organisation — and outside your control — that help or hinder your survival. Include those that now affect you and those of growing importance over the next three to five years. Categories are: Political, Economic, Social and Technological, abbreviated as P, E, S or T. You may not need every one.

Factors	Category P, E, S or T	Impact + or −	Comments

How to Plan Your Competitive Strategy

Current Corporate Organisation　　　　　　　　**Form 3**

An organisation's structure should support its purposes; 'Form follows function' as the saying goes. Analysing the strengths and weaknesses of the current organisation gives the team the understanding needed to make changes, as appropriate, to match the organisation's newly developed competitive strategic plan.

Record your ideas about all that is effective or ineffective in the current organisational structure, using the questions below as guides and adding whatever other matters are important.

1. Does the structure effectively direct and control operations; are people doing what ought to be done?

   _____
   _____
   _____

2. Is the structure efficient?

   _____
   _____
   _____

3. Are the links between functional areas effective?

   _____
   _____
   _____

4. Is the organisation too flat, or are there too many levels?

   _____
   _____
   _____

Preplanning

5. Are managers rewarded for the number of people they supervise or for effectiveness?

_____
_____
_____

6. Are there the right number of people in each functional area?

_____
_____
_____

7. Are any vital functions missing?

_____
_____
_____

8. How are changes made to the current organisation?

_____
_____
_____

How to Plan Your Competitive Strategy

Form 4

Profit and Loss Summary (000)

Percentage Increase or Decrease by Year ▶	Year %INC/ (DECR)	Year %INC/ (DECR)	Year %INC/ (DECR)	Year %INC/ (DECR)	Estimate Next Year
Net Sales					
Cost of Goods Sold					
Gross Profit					
Selling Expenses					
Gen & Admin Expenses					
TOTAL Expenses					
Operating Income					
Other Income/Expenses					
Interest Income					
Other Income					
Interest Expense					
Other Expense					
Net Profit Before Tax					
Tax					
Net Profit After Tax					
Dividends					
Depreciation					

Preplanning

Form 5

Profit and loss summary (000)

Percentage Increase or Decrease by Year ▶	Year %INC/ (DECR)	Year %INC/ (DECR)	Year %INC/ (DECR)	Year %INC/ (DECR)	Estimate Next Year
Net Sales	100%	100%	100%	100%	100%
Cost of Goods Sold					
Gross Profit					
Selling Expenses					
Gen & Admin Expenses					
TOTAL Expenses					
Operating Income					
Other Income/Expenses					
Interest Income					
Other Income					
Interest Expense					
Other Expense					
Net Profit Before Tax					
Tax					
Net Profit After Tax					
Dividends					
Depreciation					

Balance sheet summary (000)
Assets

Form 6A

For Fiscal Year ▶					Estimate for Next Year
Cash					
Marketable Securities					
Debtors (Net)					
Stock					
Prepaid Expenses					
Other Current Assets:					
Total Current Assets					
Land					
Buildings					
Less Reserve for Depreciation					
Buildings Net					
Machinery and Equipment					
Less Reserve for Depreciation					
Machinery and Equipment Net					
Other Assets					
Total Assets					

Preplanning

Balance sheet summary (000) Liabilities and net worth

Form 6B

For Fiscal Year ▶						Estimate for Next Year
Creditors						
Notes Payable						
Current Short-Term Debt						
Accrued Expenses						
Other Current						
Total Current Liabilities						
Long-Term Debt						
Total Liabilities						
Preferred Stock						
Common Stock						
Paid in Surplus						
Retained Earnings						
Total Net Worth						
Total Liabilities and Net Worth						

35

Selected financial Ratios Form

For Fiscal Year ▶						Estimate for Next Year	Industry Standards
Current Ratio (CA/CL)							
Total Debt/Net Worth							
Long-Term Debt/Net Worth							
Debtors/Sales							
Cost of Goods Sold/Stock							
Gross Profit/Sales							
Pretax Profit/Sales							
Net Profit After Tax/Sales							
Net Profit After Tax/Net Worth							
Net Profit After Tax/Total Assets							
Net Profit After Tax/Total Capital Employed							
Other Ratios Pertinent to Your Organisation							

Preplanning

Personnel Data   Form 8

For Fiscal Year ▶						Estimate for Next Year
Number of Employees: Part-time Full-time						
Total						
Average Years of Service						
Employee Turnover Rate						
Number of Employees:						
Per £ Sales						
Per £ Total Assets						
Per £ Net Profit A/T						
Wages, Salaries and Benefits:						
Average Wage Rate – Hourly						
£ Salary, Wages and Benefits/Sales						
£ Salary, Wages and Benefits/Net Profit After Taxes						

How to Plan Your Competitive Strategy

Sales Mix   Form 9

The data collected on this sheet show sales of each major product or service classified by whatever categories your organisation finds useful. For example, categories might be: major lines of business and distribution channels, market segment and customer class, or geographic area. You probably have particular categories especially for your organisation. Use a separate copy of this form for each category, listing on it all products and services appropriate to that category.

Category: _____

Products and Services Year ▶	% of Mix	% of Mix	% of Mix	% of Mix	Next Year's Est %

38

Preplanning

Market Segment Profile — Form 10

The data on this form describe the markets and market segments in which your organisation operates. Use a separate version of this form for each different market or market segment.

Market or Market Segment Description: _____

Applications or Customer Classes: _____

Channels of Distribution: _____

Year ▶					Next Year's Estimate
Market Size: Units £000					
Market Rate of Growth (% Annual Change)					
Our Share of Market: Units £000 Percentage					
Major Competitors:	Share %	Share %	Share %	Share %	Share %

How to Plan Your Competitive Strategy

Competitor Strengths and Weaknesses   **Form 11**
Use one form for each competitor/product/service combination appropriate to your organisation.

Competitor Name: _____

Product/Service: _____

1. List competitor's strengths.

   _____
   _____
   _____

2. List competitor's weaknesses.

   _____
   _____
   _____

3. What strategies is this competitor following?

   _____
   _____
   _____

4. How is your organisation responding to this competitor now – if you are – and how should you respond in the future?

   _____
   _____
   _____

Preplanning

General Organisation Data — Form 12

Every team member should answer the questions on this form on a separate piece of paper and bring them to the first meeting. The data it asks for will fuel your discussions.

1. What core competencies does your organisation have? That is, what do you do better than your competition?
2. What other strengths does the organisation have?
3. What weaknesses exist within the organisation?
4. What major opportunities do you see for your organisation in the next few years?
5. What key measurements determine the success of your organisation?
6. What difficulties do you foresee for your organisation in the next few years?
7. What changes, if any, are needed in the way your organisation is structured and managed to make it more effective in the future?
8. What company policies — written and unwritten — affect decision making; should they be changed?
9. What has been the recent strategic emphasis?
10. What are the major strategic issues to be resolved?
11. What other significant matters not noted above should the team consider when it meets?

Corporate Climate Assessment   Form 13

The questions on this form ask you to describe your organisation's climate or culture in two ways: first, the way things are done and the values most people agree on *now* and, second, the way you think things ought to be done and the values that ought to be agreed on *for the future success* of the organisation.

Listed below are a number of statements that may or may not apply to your particular organisation. Using a scale from 1 to 7 evaluate the degree to which you feel each statement characterises your organisation both now and as it needs to be in the future.

1	=	Strongly disagree; not true at all
2–3	=	Mostly not true
4	=	Neutral; sometimes true, sometimes false
5–6	=	Mostly true
7	=	Strongly agree; very true
?	=	Don't know

	Now	Future
1. Everyone knows the organisation's mission.	___	___
2. Departmental and personal objectives are set out clearly.	___	___
3. The organisation is good about communicating with its employees.	___	___
4. Operational/production systems are efficient and effective.	___	___
5. Information systems are efficient and useful.	___	___
6. People are organised in a sensible way.	___	___
7. Individual initiative and creativity are encouraged.	___	___
8. Teamwork is encouraged.	___	___
9. Management seeks input from below before making decisions.	___	___
10. We go all out to serve our customers.	___	___

Preplanning

	Now	Future
11. Customer satisfaction is measured routinely.	___	___
12. The quality of our products is excellent.	___	___
13. Our product and service are better than the competition's.	___	___
14. Product and service quality is measured routinely.	___	___
15. Quality and quality improvements are encouraged.	___	___
16. Productivity and productivity improvements are encouraged.	___	___
17. The organisation encourages innovation.	___	___
18. The organisation is aggressive, willing to take risks.	___	___
19. The organisation has exciting new products in progress.	___	___
20. Management has focus. It knows where it is going.	___	___
21. Management responds when there is a problem.	___	___
22. Management anticipates. We plan ahead.	___	___
23. Management implements well.	___	___
24. Long-term profitability drives the organisation.	___	___
25. Morale is good; the company has team spirit.	___	___
26. Compensation is fair and competitive.	___	___
27. Where appropriate, effective incentive compensation programmes are in place.	___	___
28. Benefits are good.	___	___
29. Working conditions are pleasant.	___	___
30. There is good opportunity for personal growth and career development.	___	___
31. Employees are provided with the tools and training to do their jobs.	___	___
32. Employees generally feel secure in their jobs.	___	___

How to Plan Your Competitive Strategy

	Now	Future
33. We are ethical in our treatment of employees and customers.	___	___
34. The organisation and its employees contribute to the community.	___	___

Step 2
Intelligence Gathering

Gathering information

Gathering data about your customers, your company, your competition, and the world in which you operate can be time consuming but it is enormously rewarding. A realistic understanding of where you stand in relation to all these elements is fundamental to acting wisely in the future. Do the job carefully remembering that inaccurate data can be lethal to your organisation.

Case study

> **The importance of data**
> The manufacturers of small- to medium-sized capital goods sold a significant part of their product line through independent agents. Because of their arrangement with the agents, they did not normally have data about the ultimate consumer of this part of their sales. When they tried to determine what drove demand for their products, this lack of data made their information incomplete in this critical area and prevented the team from drawing meaningful insights. A simple alteration of their arrangement solved the problem for the future but they could never recover the history they had lost.

Data vs intelligence

Individual facts such as the value of a shipment, the postcode of a customer, or the stock number of a product are *data*. By themselves, these facts are not very useful, but when they are collected and focused, they become *intelligence*. Total shipment values can be gross sales, a collection of customers with the same postcode can indicate the size of a geographic market segment, and total sales by item can show which products are selling well or badly.

Use your experience to decide whether or not the data elements listed on your team members' worksheets in Chapter 1 will yield useful intelligence. Add others that make sense to you and delete – thoughtfully – those that have no bearing on your business. Decide what you want to learn before you start gathering data.

As you translate data into intelligence, be thorough and try not to make judgements just yet. The interesting thing about intelligence gathering is that unbiased data gathering often yields surprising conclusions.

Case study

> ### An unexpected finding
> A medium-sized construction company operated branches in cities throughout the United States. A major source of concern to management was the large profitability variations among branches. Traditional company thinking held that the variability was due almost entirely to individual branch manager quality. They instituted extensive management training programmes to solve this (perceived) problem.
>
> However, when they initiated a market analysis of their business, highlighting the type of work performed, it became apparent that some branches concentrated on a few types while others tried to be 'all things to all people'. Further analysis confirmed that those who were more focused generally possessed a strong core competence; their results showed greater customer satisfaction and, not coincidentally, better profits. Apparently, the issue was not quality of

> management as much as the ability to develop and focus on specific core competencies.
>
> While this was, in a sense, a management issue, it was very specific and much easier to address than the broad range of management skills previously under study.
>
> A long-term competitive strategy founded on developing and focusing on individual branch core competencies quickly led to profit improvement as the poorly performing branches learned to focus as well as their more successful counterparts.

How much is enough?
The worksheets provided in this book are based on broad experience with many companies. The intelligence they ask for is usually enough for an average organisation.

If, during the intelligence gathering phase, you find some data hard, expensive or even impossible to get, begin with the best estimates you can develop internally. Then wait until analysis or discussion indicates that more exact information is critical and worth taking extraordinary pains to gather before spending time and money to get it.

Where to find information
Begin with formal company records such as the annual report, regular periodic reports and the records kept by responsible managers on such matters as maintenance expenses, brand sales and employee turnover. This kind of intelligence is particularly straightforward in the financial area.

Many other items of intelligence such as opportunities, constraints, problems, corporate climate and external influences come from personal observations as you work with customers, fellow employees and suppliers. Sometimes, insights come from reading or watching television. Formal records tend to reflect history; observations about the world around us let us know where we are and suggest new directions.

How to Plan Your Competitive Strategy

Often, companies have a great deal of data that simply needs to be gathered and analysed, such as customer suggestions or complaints, sales trends, exit interviews and the like. If you can be clear about what you want to know, it is surprising how often you can find the information to answer your questions. Customer suggestions, for example, have always been fertile sources of new product ideas; exit interviews point to organisational problems.

You may need professional help or training when you want objectivity — as you would in surveying employees — or if you have a large group to work with. However, much can be done with the resources on hand. For example, if you want to know how many customers buy more than twice a year, you could find out by looking at a year's worth of sales records or by sampling selected customers — which takes some expertise but is fast, cheap and remarkably accurate.

Intelligence Gathering Planning Worksheet

In your current workplace or situation, assume you have been assigned to a team to gather information in your area. How would you answer the following questions?

1. I am responsible for gathering intelligence in these areas:

_____

_____

_____

2. Major questions to be answered are:

_____

_____

_____

Intelligence Gathering

3. I will need these kinds of data:

   _____

   _____

   _____

4. This is where I expect to find the data and how I plan to gather it:

   _____

   _____

   _____

5. These people will help me; their assignments appear beside their names:

   _____

   _____

   _____

Step 3
Analysis

The two-level approach

Information analysis takes hard thinking and some imagination to produce the kinds of result useful in forming competitive strategy. A two-level approach works best.

Level 1 has each subject expert (SE), such as a marketing manager or the head of finance, first analyse the intelligence gathered about their area, using experience to understand the material and draw conclusions. These results are written down and shared among the team.

Level 2 has the team gather in a one-day meeting to present their conclusions for everybody to discuss. (*Note:* All team members will be SEs but not all SEs will be team members; for example, the company solicitor or the economist might be SEs but not on the team.) This approach uses SE expertise to screen intelligence into useful conclusions and invites team members from other disciplines to examine these conclusions critically, using their general business knowledge and particular point of view. The aim is to avoid blind spots that come from familiarity with an area.

Level 1. Subject expert's data analysis

Each subject expert, knowing what is important in their particular area, gathers and analyses intelligence to get the answers the organisation needs. The marketing manager must find out, for example, who the customers are, what they buy, and how satisfied they are — to name just a few of the many questions that need answering. Much of this kind of intelligence will be part of an SE's regular job and will be gathered routinely by the SE's staff.

Identifying SWOTs
For their own areas, SEs must identify four elements:

Strengths	What we should be doing that we already do well
Weaknesses	What we should be doing that we fail to do well
Opportunities	Areas where we can expand or improve
Threats	From competition, government, etc, that we must respond to but cannot prevent.

Use the code word 'SWOT' to remember this list.

Every SE should be clear about the organisation's current *strengths* and *weaknesses*, at least in his or her area of responsibility. These understandings must be written down for the whole planning team.

In addition, SEs must think about *opportunities*: the marketing manager, for example, should have ideas and intelligence about new products, new markets and new customers; the production manager should have ideas about productivity; the human resources manager should be thinking about the best ways to hire and train employees in the future. Although much is unknown when we talk about new directions, every SE should at least have reasonable ideas about areas to be researched and approaches to data gathering.

Threats can be identified in either of two ways:

- Known activities such as lawsuits, regulations or competitive initiatives; or
- Problems that might reasonably happen such as strikes at

contract negotiating time, bills before Parliament or the loss of a key manager. Also consider natural disasters such as floods, droughts, etc. We call this 'creative worrying'.

An SE's experience and ingenuity will suggest ways of dealing with visible threats as well as with those that are unseen but that can reasonably be expected.

Identifying PESTs
Opportunities and threats (the O and T of SWOT) can be found within and outside the company. Most come from four areas outside the organisation's control: Political, Economic, Social and Technological. Use the code word PEST to remember this list. Each area may threaten the enterprise or present opportunities. For example:

Political	Political realities such as treaties, a new council, EU Directives or Acts of Parliament
Economic	Economic factors such as the relation of the pound to foreign currency, interest rates and unemployment levels
Social	Social trends such as the ageing of the workforce, sentiment against smoking, the green movement and immigration
Technological	Technological changes like the declining cost of computing power, the increase of mobile telephone availability and video conferencing.

When you write about opportunities and threats, group them according to the PEST list and note whether they come from inside or outside the company; this will make it easy for the team to understand and think about them.

The chief executive's PEST analysis should take the broadest possible view in order to discern outside influences likely to affect the business in the years to come. This analysis often produces some of the most significant intelligence the team has to address.

Case study

> **PEST analysis**
> A medium-sized regional bank, serving an essentially rural community, focused on face-to-face, highly personal service as their primary competitive strategy. Their PEST analysis identified several trends that suggested the need for an additional strategy. In recent years, the characteristics of their marketplace had changed to reflect an influx of suburban and urban people seeking 'the better life'. These people brought a culture and background to the market different from that of traditional customers. They expected technological sophistication from their bank. At the same time, home computing was on the increase as well as the ability to communicate between home computers and the bank.
>
> As they came to understand these developments, the bank team realised that in addition to its branch-oriented face-to-face strategy, it needed a technological strategy. Such a strategy would serve newcomers to the market and their probable demand for electronic banking as opposed to the historic, leisurely, personal approach.
>
> Without this alteration in strategy – which would entail significant internal culture shifts – the organisation would probably be unable to retain its major share of the market.

Level 2. Members' analysis session

When every SE has collected data in his or her area and extracted intelligence from it, the whole team meets for an analysis session. This meeting will take at least a day and may take more depending on the amount of material to be analysed and the number of people on the team. At this meeting, as at the off-site meeting that comes later, individual team members must play two parts at the same time. Primarily, they must be concerned with what is best for the company *as a whole*, while also representing their *area of expertise* (finance, marketing, production, and the like). Corporate thinking is usually the harder of these two. It is critical that all managers learn to play both parts, that is, to think strategically, by the time they gather off-site to build the strategic plan.

As the SEs present their material, consider these matters:

- Do the hard data and the intelligence derived from it challenge cherished beliefs? After all, reality-based planning is the only kind that succeeds. Be especially alert to surprises and investigate them thoroughly.
- Determine those factors critical to the success of anyone in your business, those few things — usually no more than half a dozen — that you *must* do well in order to succeed. For example, a car manufacturer must be concerned with styling, a dealer network and cost control.
- Identify the strengths that help your company to succeed, that is, those things which distinguish you as an enterprise in the minds of your customers. These are your core competencies. Match them with the critical success factors for your kind of business to be sure that you have at least a minimum of competency in every critical area, although you may possess additional strengths as well.
- Identify the corporate weaknesses likely to impinge on those factors critical for success.
- Come to agreement on what the financial analysis means.
- Understand the market analysis and develop tentative strategies by market segment.
- Learn what the competition is doing and incorporate this intelligence into your tentative strategies.
- Address all PEST (Political, Economic, Social and Technological) issues in the light of their impact on the company.

Teams find it productive to deal with *internal analysis* ahead of *external analysis*; and then they consider *threats* before *opportunities*. This sequence makes the consideration of opportunities a transition from analysis to planning competitive strategies.

Often, this session produces significant questions that suggest additional data gathering and analysis by individual SEs. Here too, the team may decide to invest time and money

Analysis

gathering specific additional data originally felt to be too expensive or troublesome.

Prepare a loose-leaf notebook for each participant that includes the material presented by each individual modified on the basis of the team discussion. (We will call this 'background intelligence'.) Additionally, be sure to include a copy of all conclusions, discussion notes and tentative new directions from flip charts and blackboards (covering internal and external business analyses, threats and opportunities). Suggested tabs for your Competitive Strategy Planning Notebook — First Meeting are:

- Background Intelligence
- Internal Business Analysis
- External Business Analysis
- Threats/Opportunities.

(*Note*. Other tabs will be added for the next team meeting).

Finally, all team members go back to their workplace and use this notebook, their personal notes and their recollection of the meeting to develop ideas about solutions, initiatives and insights into things as they really are.

A word about the analysis meeting

A great deal of concentrated thinking has to be accomplished here, and most people will find it a challenge to be alert throughout the whole meeting. The agenda outline shown here allots time proportioned for each segment of a single-day meeting. Note that if the team is large or the material complex, the meeting might take longer. The director of the meeting must watch the clock, dividing the time fairly among participants and topics, not forgetting breaks for refreshments and lunch. Notice that in a one-day meeting for a team of six, each person has only half an hour (within the Background Intelligence segment) for presentation and team commentary.

First Meeting Agenda Outline

- Purpose of Meeting by chief executive (½ hr)
- Background Intelligence Presentations by SEs and Team Commentary (3 1/2 hrs)

—*Lunch Break*—

- Discussion: Internal Business Analysis (1 hr)
- Discussion: External Business Analysis (1½ hrs)
- Discussion: Threats/Opportunities (1½ hrs)
- Next Steps, Assignments, and Conclusion (½ hr)

Analysis Worksheet

For your records, list the areas of expertise in your organisation and then write the name of the SE for each area. After your Analysis Meeting, write out your responses to the following questions:

1. What SWOTs (Strengths, Weaknesses, Opportunities and Threats) exist in your area of expertise?

_____
_____
_____

2. What SWOTs do you see in the company outside your area of expertise?

_____
_____
_____

Analysis

3. What are the PEST (Political, Economic, Social and Technological) opportunities and threats in your area of expertise?

   _____
   _____
   _____
   _____

4. What are the PEST opportunities and threats *outside* your area of expertise?

   _____
   _____
   _____
   _____

5. After the Analysis Meeting, I've found I need to gather more intelligence about these areas:

   _____
   _____
   _____
   _____

Step 4
Building the Plan

Preparing for the planning session

After the local analysis meeting, the team gathers off-site to build the competitive strategy plan. We recommend going off-site, as experience shows that planning sessions held on-site tempt participants to try conducting some business as usual; the telephone is an especially troublesome interruption. When planning competitive strategy is new and difficult, managers find it more comfortable to retreat into familiar tasks. Nevertheless, some organisations must – or feel they must – plan competitive strategy locally.

In such cases, it is vital to success that the director ask the team to establish rules about when and how messages can be delivered to participants and when and for how long managers can leave the meeting. A useful arrangement for messages is to have a message board *outside* the meeting room where messages wait until the teams takes a break. In addition, the chief executive can establish a norm of handling business outside the session by setting an example of only taking or making calls during breaks and meals.

Advantages of off-site meetings

Managers who have never experienced an off-site meeting may think of such sessions as vacations or rewards, that is, places where no one works very hard and where there is a little too much to eat and drink. Perhaps this is true of gatherings designed specifically to reward performance but Competitive Strategy Planning Sessions differ profoundly from this stereotype.

Competitive Strategy Planning Sessions focus on working out the future of the organisation in a process that absorbs the time and energy of participants. It is not unusual to find groups gathering in the evening, compelled by the day's discussion to revisit or expand on their conclusions. They rework their numbers to be sure that they can deliver what they promised. These sessions work best away from headquarters for several reasons.

First, the team is away from interruptions. The daily business of running the company leaves little time for strategic thinking. Urgent tasks with deadlines always pre-empt important tasks since the latter usually have no deadlines. At the off-site session, there is nothing to do but think strategically and everyone needed is there. So, the work gets done.

Besides, if absolutely necessary, there is always the telephone and fax machine.

Second, the off-site environment encourages the management team members to see themselves as part of a larger whole. Every individual on the planning team, except the chief executive, must act in two capacities to make the Competitive Strategy Planning Session successful. Each must represent his or her own area of the company (finance, production, etc) as well as consider what is best for the entire company. Often, the CE's point of view is new even to senior-level managers who have spent years in particular disciplines and who normally negotiate with one another for people and money. Moving the session away from the office gives everyone a fresh start and an imperative to work for what is best for the business rather than what is best for their division.

The planning session

This meeting can take from two to four days depending on the complexity of the business and the size of the team. By this time, the team has gathered whatever additional intelligence was needed and has thought about the values, policies and culture of the organisation. Shown here is a sample agenda for a three-day meeting. You might need to adjust the schedule somewhat for your organisation to ensure that each element gets the time it requires and address all topics.

DAY 1	DAY 2	DAY 3
Purpose of Meeting by CE	Critical Success Factors and Key Result Areas	Tactics and Action Plans (cont)
Presentations and Discussion of New Intelligence Since Last Meeting	Goals	Controls
	Strategies	Sharing the Vision
Values, Culture and Policies	Tactics and Action Plans	Conclusion
Vision		
Mission		

At the outset of this meeting, additional notebook tabs (the first four were provided at the first meeting) should be provided as follows:

- Values/Culture/Policies
- Vision
- Mission
- Critical Success Factors
- Key Result Areas
- Goals
- Strategies
- Tactics and Action Plans
- Controls
- Sharing the Vision.

Participants can file in this notebook all material gathered for the planning session and all material developed during this session and the last. When complete, the notebook contains your organisation's competitive strategy and tactics plus all the intelligence and thinking behind it: a valuable asset that is probably *company confidential*.

Values, policies and culture

When the team returns to the workplace to implement the tactics determined at this meeting, they need to be clear about the organisation's 'shalts' and 'shalt nots'. That is, what most people believe is important (*values*), those things we do not do (*policies*), and therefore, what kind of a group we are (*culture*). If tactics do not fit culture, you and your people will not execute them.

Values are things like:

- Level of quality
- Level of service
- Organisational purpose
- Style
- Attitude towards employees
- How hard we work
- Integrity.

Policies are limits on activity like:

- Operating in the continent of Europe only
- Not doing business with the government
- Always choosing the low bidder.

Values plus policies equals culture: the kind of organisation we are. Some organisations take time in this meeting to develop a creed (which differs from the mission statement described later in this chapter because a creed describes the beliefs of the great majority of the people in the organisation while a mission statement is strictly business).

Vision

The turbulence of daily living and working absorbs our attention and distracts us from important goals. Urgent things with deadlines that have to be done soon (the weekly report, making a presentation) crowd out important things that usually have no deadlines (learn a foreign language, make a will, establish a research facility). A clear vision steadily reminds us of our long-range goals and ambitions, giving us a star to steer by.

Why a vision is important
Your vision describes where the team wants their organisation to be at some future time, say ten years from now. The exact number of years is not as important as choosing a point distant enough so that the team can think about the organisation relatively free from current concerns. Experience shows that too short a time frame for the vision usually leads to something that is essentially nothing more than an improved version of the current situation — not the quantum leap forward necessary to energise the organisation. A vision should say something about these topics, usually in a fairly general way. Before beginning, you might want to read the example given below.

Here is an example of the full-length vision statement for a hypothetical company, Contrex Custom Devices plc.

Contrex Custom Devices plc
Vision 2005

1. **Sales volume and profitability.** By the year 2005 Contrex will gross £165m in sales (35–40% government and 60–65% private industry); net profits of 12%.
2. **Markets to be served.** Contrex will continue to serve vehicle manufacturers such as cars, aircraft, trucks, power boats, and mass transit.
3. **Products/services to be offered.** We will design and manufacture custom sub-assemblies using standard elements (motors, fasteners, connectors, etc) when possible.
4. **Relation to customers and the marketplace.** Our *customers* will expect us to solve difficult engineering problems by blending a broad range of expertise in all engineering disciplines with considerable creativity — we will always be designing and piloting things that have never been built before. We will extend the efforts of (and compete with) customer in-house engineering.

   We will differentiate ourselves in the *marketplace* by being the best at producing novel and highly useful products that can, subsequently, be manufactured at reasonable cost; we will charge a premium for design work but price manufactured products competitively.

Building the Plan

5. **Number and types of employees.** Our scientist/engineer/designer teams will continue to be the core of the business; by 2005 there will be 10–12 teams of 6–8 people each. Administrative management will be minimised and should grow no larger than one manager for every 10 design team people – this includes all levels of management, especially top management. Manufacturing management should stabilise at about 30 and production workers at 400.
6. **Core competencies to keep or establish.** Our core competence will be solving function problems made difficult by constraints of space, temperature, cost, or time, for example, using effective teams of inter-disciplinary members with a talent for creative thinking.

This full-length vision, after additional input and editing, should be communicated throughout the company. Keep and publish this full-length vision. Your people make decisions all day long based on available facts and influenced by their own values. Their behaviour can be represented by this diagram:

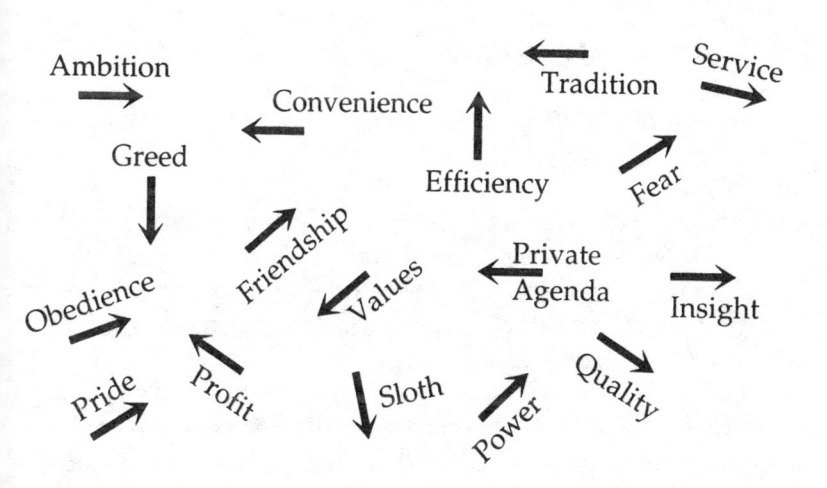

Decision making without a corporate vision

The organisation with a unifying vision looks like this single arrow (representing the vision) that contains the employees' individual arrows *all pointing in the same direction.*

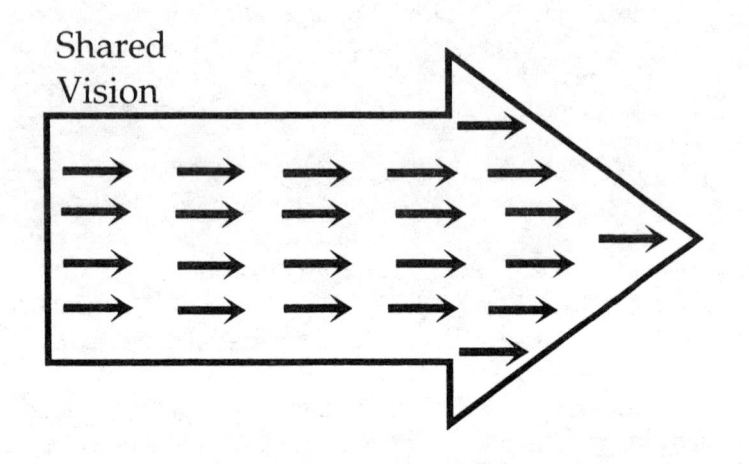

Shared Vision

Decision making with a corporate vision.

An effective vision guides everybody's decisions every day and has these characteristics:

- **Leader initiated**. Top management's job is to develop the company's vision; no one else can or will do this.
- **Shared and supported**. Everyone must understand the vision; it cannot be a management secret (remember the arrows).
- **Comprehensive and detailed**. Details make a vision concrete even when broadly stated.
- **Positive and inspiring**. The more important and uplifting the vision, the more people will be energised by it and willing to stretch to meet its goals.

Another characteristic of visions is that they often contain values, as in this part of General Electric's vision: 'A passion for excellence; a hatred of bureaucracy'.

If time and talent allow, someone on your team could

Building the Plan

produce a short, memorable, inspiring version that emphasises the main points of the vision. For example, using the Contrex statement given in the full-length example, the short version might be:

> *Contrex will grow and prosper, delighting its customers by producing elegant solutions to very difficult technical problems using a team-based approach that combines wide technical expertise and experience with practical creativity. And we will manufacture what we design.*

Robert Townsend of AVIS produced this short version: 'We want to become the fastest growing company with the highest profit margins in the business of renting and leasing vehicles without drivers.' Ironically, when they finished clarifying their vision, AVIS got out of the taxi and limousine business because these involved vehicles with drivers.

Sometimes a vision can be summarised in a slogan, both memorable and effective. One such example is Jan Carlzon's dubbing of *Scandinavian Airlines* as 'The businessman's airline'. Another is the Ford Motor Company's motto, 'Quality is job one'.

But, never start by writing your vision as a slogan. Rather, first address the specifics outlined above. Then, after team agreement on those specifics, distil what you have written into a slogan that captures the essence of the specifics and can be easily understood by all employees. Remember, though, that not all visions can be distilled into effective slogans nor do all companies want to try.

In short, the vision you develop is a compact statement about where you are taking the company. The mission statement described later in this section tells how you will make the trip.

See *101 Great Mission Statements* by Timothy R V Foster, published by Kogan Page, for further suggestions.

Developing a vision

Some visions articulate, perhaps for the first time, a shared understanding of a future that everyone wants. Other visions paint a whole new picture that only a few had seen before. A few visions are the work of one entrepreneur, but more often they are framed by a team. However it arises, a fully formed vision should be agreed by the whole management team. This section describes the process of team visioning.

We have already discussed how to consider such areas as the company's sales and profit margins, the products the company will make, the markets it will serve and what share of each market it will enjoy. Additionally discussed were the company's relation to customers and marketplace, the size of the company in terms of employees, the corporate climate and core competencies the corporation will need in order to achieve that vision.

There are many ways to organise vision development. One recommended approach divides the entire team into sub-teams of three people each (being sure that each sub-team contains different personalities and different functional points of view). Give each sub-team between one and two hours to address the various areas noted above. Reconvene and have each sub-team present its conclusions to the entire group. This method ensures that each person has had an active part in developing the vision.

Once the full team has heard all reports, they usually find great similarity among them. When differences remain after discussion, the chief executive exercises the leadership role of that office and makes a decision while being careful to explain to the entire team the rationale behind it. This approach usually retains full-team commitment. Finally, select one member from each sub-team and assign that group the job of drafting the final version of the detailed vision.

Once the detailed vision has been completed and agreed to, designate a further sub-team to rework the vision into a form appropriate for communication to all employees as the organisation's official vision. Keep this version true to the detailed vision and add inspiration by including some or all of these elements: achievement, recognition, responsibility, worthwhile work and personal growth.

Mission

Your mission statement tells what business you are in and how you plan to act every day – that is, excellently – to achieve your vision. It is the essential counterweight to the ten-year vision: Visioning without acting is just dreaming and acting without a vision can lead anywhere. Both together will take your company wherever the team wants to lead it. Where vision provides a long-term focus, mission directs the organisation for the next three to five years, recognising what needs to be done immediately to achieve the objectives of the vision.

Generally, the mission should state these things:

- What business you are in
- Customers
- Products and services.

Here is an example of a well-thought-out mission statement (examples follow in parentheses):

A mission statement

The mission of Smith Corporation is to become the dominant supplier of user-installed aftermarket automotive products (*the business*). Our customers own small- and medium-sized vehicles of both domestic and foreign manufacture (*customers*). We will achieve dominance by offering products that combine ease of installation with competitive quality and are sold at an above-average price. These will include performance-improvement equipment, tools, novelties such as comfort items and appearance enhancers (*products and services*). Our unique competence will be an unsurpassed understanding of the needs of our customers and this will drive everything we do.

What business you are in
Be particularly careful deciding what business you are in. The US railroads got into trouble by limiting themselves to the railroad business; when they understood that they were in the

transportation business, we began to see piggyback trucks on flatcars and a return to profitability. Professional sports teams understand they are in the entertainment business, which broadens their scope of activity. On the other hand, beware of broad definitions that provide little direction to the organisation. A distillery defining itself as being in the 'beverage' business could devote resources to investigating coffee, tea or milk – probably not good diversifications. In this case, a phrase like 'social beverages' probably would be more meaningful.

Customers. Be clear about your customers so that everything you plan to do gives them the same reassuring message: 'This company sells your kind of product/service'.

Selecting the customers you intend to serve can be your most significant decision. It is part of a circular process in which core competencies determine initial products or services... which defines customers... who in turn suggest additional products and services. And these new products or services may require changes in core competencies. All together, these determine the shape of the company: staffing, organisation, strategies, even location. You must be clear about who your customers are, that you can reach them, that what you offer them fills real needs both now and in the future, and finally, that you can bring them these things at a price they can and will pay in preference to competing methods of satisfying their needs.

Products and services. Similarly, be alert to the need to offer new products and services but be certain you truly understand whatever business you enter. New products, mergers and acquisitions have been the downfall of many companies that did not know what they were getting into.

Critical success factors and key result areas
In Step 3, Analysis subject experts were asked to identify the factors critical for your business. These are those few things your company – in fact any company in your business – must do well to prosper. Key result areas (KRAs) describe what you

will measure in your company to be sure of satisfying the imperatives of these critical success factors.

If a steady stream of new products is critical to your business, for example, everything about new products could become key result areas to be measured periodically. For example, this could be the number of new product ideas submitted to a screening committee, the number of new products introduced to the marketplace every year and new product success. However, organisations do best when they concentrate on a few strategic KRAs and leave subordinate KRAs to functional managers. In this new product example, a single KRA summarising what the team wants to measure might be product mix – what percentage of our product line is less than two years old and what is the profitability of those new products?

When the company performs well in meeting the requirements of a KRA, it needs to keep up the good work. But when your company's performance differs from what a KRA study suggests is optimal, strategic attention is needed. For these areas, establish measurable ideal objectives as planning targets. For instance, an objective might be that new products make up half the product mix within the next two years.

Goals

The next step is to see what goals the team can commit to. Attempt to set realistic goals for the next three to five years for your organisation. Build some stretch into your goals – organisations sometimes tend to underachieve. With your goals as a guide, the data you gather will provide useful intelligence about progress or the lack of it.

Using the chart *Competitive Strategy Development: From Critical Success Factor to Action Plans* (provided on page 70) as an example, you can see the progression from a single critical success factor to a set of action plans. (Use this chart while reading the rest of this section to understand how competitive strategies develop from the general to the specific in a logical flow.)

How to Plan Your Competitive Strategy

Competitive Strategy Development: From Critical Success Factor to Action Plans (New Products)

Critical Success Factor	Key Result Area and Measures	Strategy	Tactics	Action Plans
Continuous successful new product introductions	Product mix (what percentage of product line is less than two years old? What is profit contribution of new products?)	Increase number of successful new products in the product mix by learning to understand what the market wants and needs	Focus employees on new product identification and development	Set up profit sharing system
			Listen actively to customers	Refine development process in R & D
			Understand marketplace	Establish screening committee
			Watch competitive product offering	Train product managers in development and introduction of new products
			Establish new product oversight committee	Set up routine competitive data gathering process
				Establish intelligence recording system
				Establish score-keeping system
				Set up focus groups

Read this example from left to right remembering that these lists are not exhaustive.

Notice that the Critical Success Factor generates a single strategic Key Result Area which, in turn, leads to a single Strategy. Strategies tell, at a policy level, *what* is to be done; Tactics say, more specifically, *how* Strategies are to be executed. Thus, one Strategy can lead to several Tactics, and each Tactic can lead to many Action Plans. Action Plans are the six-month (or less) projects that execute Tactics and Strategies and fulfil the goals of Key Result Areas.

Since new products is the key result area in our example, goals might include, among others:

- The number of products introduced within the last 16 months as a percentage of all active products
- The profitability of new products compared with established products
- The number of new products in the development pipeline.

These goals form the basis for all future plans and must be endorsed by the team, especially the managers, responsible for specific results.

The sub-team approach recommended to develop the vision, discussed earlier in this section, can be useful in goal setting. Divided into sub-teams, all team members become active participants in the goal-setting process, thereby ensuring involvement and commitment by the leaders of the various sections of the organisation. Make sure that all goals are established as 'our goals' by the managers involved.

Strategies

Strategies say *what* you are going to do to achieve the goals set in your key result areas, and tactics say *how* you are going to do it. Typically, each goal requires a separate strategy unless creativity or luck combine to allow one strategy to achieve more than a single goal. For example, if your goal is for new products to represent half of your product mix within two years, then a strategy might be:

> *Develop processes for identifying, developing and bringing to market profitable new products that fit our mission; support this effort with appropriate people and resources.*

Strategies are, by nature, established at a general level. At this stage in the process, you are identifying areas where priority effort must be expended (new product development) and directing the nature of that effort (developing processes and allocating resources).

As a rule, there should be few strategies – five to seven are usual. That is not to say that these are the only things the team has identified as being desirable to do. Rather, it says that, of the many things identified, these are the few things likely to make the greatest difference and therefore the things to which the organisation will devote its scarce resources. An overwhelming tendency is to undertake too many strategies. It is hard to decide not to do something which, on the surface, seems desirable – prioritising strategies fully tests the mettle of management. A competitive strategic plan that undertakes more work than the resources of the company can support is a recipe for failure.

Tactics and action plans

Since tactics are the *how* of planning, be specific about exactly what is to be done to realise every strategy. Tactics for the new product strategy presented in our example might be divided into:

- Identifying new products
- Developing promising new product ideas
- Bringing new products to market.

There will always be at least one tactic to support each strategy and often more. Similarly, each tactic leads to one or more action plans. Action plans are defined as the projects the organisation will undertake to shape its future. Action plans have three parts:

1. A description of the plan connecting it to the tactic, strategy, goal and key result area, and critical success factor that it supports
2. A schedule of major tasks with target dates and individual responsibilities
3. Estimates of the time and money required over the life of the action plan and the expected payback over some appropriate period, such as the next three to five years.

Building the Plan

The tactic of identifying new products might generate a single action plan or several action plans depending on the size of the effort. As a rule, action plans should take no more than six months to accomplish and shorter plans are better. Your team's knowledge of the realities of your business must guide you.

In the period between this meeting and the next, the teams responsible for executing the action plans identified here will use the worksheets provided in this book to describe each action plan fully (by identifying it, laying out its major milestones, and presenting its costs and benefits). For now, at this off-site meeting, the title of each action plan, a brief description, and best estimates of target dates, costs and benefits are sufficient. When the planning team returns to the workplace, these must be refined and the worksheets completed by the people who will implement those action plans. Once again, the team concept ensures the involvement and commitment so essential to successful achievement. Where an action plan affects multiple functions within the organisation, ensure that the team preparing the plan has members from each affected function.

All members of the planning team commit to championing action plans in their area of organisational responsibility. First, each champion selects teams to develop action plans in the champion's area of responsibility. Once an action plan has been approved, the champion will provide resources for the project managers responsible for each action plan, clear away red tape, and display a continuing interest in project progress. As an example, the first action plan in developing a competitive strategy for your organisation is conducting a strategic planning session. The CE is champion, and the coordinator is project manager.

The sum of all action plans

Once all the assigned teams have written their action plans in the period following this off-site session, the planning team will reconvene to review these plans. (This session is best held

How to Plan Your Competitive Strategy

on-site so that action plan project managers can present their plans and answer questions without having to travel.) At this session, the team focuses on the following questions:

- Does each action plan effectively address the strategies and goals it is designed to implement?
- Are the steps, schedules and requirements for people and money realistic?
- Can all action plans together be staffed and funded from available resources or do some need to be delayed until key resources are free?
- When all action plans are consolidated, does the resulting financial outlook for the organisation make sense?

A useful tool for addressing the last question is the Action Plan Matrix (see page 78), which shows the sum of all action plans for the next three years. The director makes a large matrix on the wall of the conference room using a chalkboard or flipchart. Then the director simply lists all action plans.

Next, the team determines the company's base business for each of the next three years – that is, the business that can be expected without special efforts such as the strategies and tactics discussed at the off-site meeting. Put these three values on a flipchart.

As each action plan is presented and discussed, record on the matrix its costs, benefits and net value (the difference between costs and benefits). When all action plans have been presented, add all net values to the base business year by year and see if the action plans meet the goals set at the off-site meeting. For safety, total values should exceed goals by at least 25–30 per cent. If they fall short, more action plans are required. If resources and time are limited, goals might have to be revised.

Some kinds of action plan have costs only. These arise, for example, from the need to comply with government regulations.

Controls

Controls measure progress and tell if you are winning or losing. They are the data that give you decision-making information. Near the end of this three-day session, the team needs to develop and agree on a system of controls:

- Action plan controls (presented in Step 6: Control and Follow-Up) will tell you whether spending is going according to plan or progress is going according to schedule but say nothing about how effective the results of the project may be.
- Goals measure the results of executing tactics (that is, one or more action plans) as part of a strategy, and tell how well each tactic is accomplishing what it was designed to do.

The control system, managed by the coordinator, should include a procedure for keeping the planning team informed and having them meet periodically to review progress. The purpose of such a meeting is twofold: to evaluate progress and to make decisions, as necessary. Inevitably, actual results deviate from plans. The team must address variations and decide when action is required. Hold such meetings monthly until the team decides that less frequent meetings will be adequate.

Sharing the vision

Planning competitive strategy is mainly the responsibility of senior management but executing it is everybody's job. The last step in this off-site meeting must be to plan a strategy for sharing the vision and mission with everyone in the organisation. Typically, employees worry about what has been going on at this senior-level meeting; you must let them know immediately what has been decided and what it means to them. Many will be involved in implementing action plans. Some of the information will be corporate confidential, but keep everyone informed of plans and progress as far as possible. Use what you have discovered about the organisation's climate to help in sharing information effectively.

Building the Plan: A Preparation Worksheet

Prepare yourself for the off-site meeting by answering these questions.

1. What are the company's core values?
   _____
   _____

2. What are the company's core policies?
   _____
   _____

3. What kind of organisation do we belong to?
   _____
   _____

4. What business are we in?
   _____
   _____

5. What are our products or services, and to whom do we sell?
   _____
   _____

6. What would you like to see in the company's vision?
   _____
   _____

7. What should the company's mission be, day to day?
   _____
   _____

Building the Plan

8. Every company in our business must do well in a few areas to survive and prosper; these are:

   _____

   _____

9. Key result areas for our particular business and goals for those areas are:

   _____

   _____

10. I will propose that our core strategies be:

    _____

    _____

11. Effective tactics to accomplish the goals of these strategies should be:

    _____

    _____

12. The names of proposed action plans associated with each of these tactics and the project managers who might be assigned to them are:

    _____

    _____

13. Useful ways of sharing all the team developments with the rest of the company are:

    _____

    _____

How to Plan Your Competitive Strategy

Action Plan Matrix (000)

Name of Action Plan	Person Resp	First Year				Second Year				Third Year			
		Gross Sales	Profit	Add'l Expn	Cap £ Needed	Add'l People Needed	Gross Sales	Profit	Add'l Expn	Cap £ Needed	Add'l People Needed	Gross Sales	Profit	Add'l Expn	Cap £ Needed	Add'l People Needed
TOTALS:													

Step 5
Implementation

Managing projects

Planning is about what we will do *now* to make the *future* what we want it to be, thus implementation of action plans is the critical next step in executing competitive strategy. Action plan projects need championing because many fall outside people's regular duties; they need a special kind of management since projects differ from routine administrative work in important ways.

Of course, some jobs actually consist largely of projects that fit the description of an action plan, such as software development or new project introduction, but even the people in such jobs will find action plans replacing or being added to current assignments.

This part of the book presents ideas about managing projects. Although the projects described in your action plans will vary in complexity, the concepts described in this section apply to all projects. The difference is that the more complex the project, the more strictly these concepts should be adhered to and documented. Whereas simple projects can usually be managed well with action plan worksheets alone, for complex projects, use project management software to establish and maintain schedule control rather than simply relying on worksheets.

How to Plan Your Competitive Strategy

Project work vs routine work

Key elements of project work are deadlines, novelty, pressure and change. Key elements of normal work are regularity, efficiency and fluctuating pressure. The table below suggests other differences.

Project work	Routine work
Definite start and end	Continuous process
Well-defined objective	Periodic deliverables
Unique product	Routine product
High pressure	Varying pressure
Team of many skills	Fewer skills in work group
Method plus creativity more valuable than business experience	Business experience most valuable
Cuts across organisational boundaries	One organisation
Team concentrates on goals	Must deal with all staff issues
Frequent change	Moderate change
Staff assigned only for project duration	Permanent staff
Project manager might not have direct authority over all resources needed	Most resources required are contained in unit

© Alfred B Hurd

What project managers do

Projects are undertaken when it is important to do something new — efficiency comes later. Project managers:

- Plan the project and replan as necessary to account for changes in scope, resources or team members.

Implementation

- See that the work gets done on schedule; this is the part of the job most like general management.
- Build and work closely with the project team whose members often come from areas outside the project manager's expertise.
- Connect the project with their own management, usually the planning team champion.
- Serve the project's customer intelligently, constantly managing change and expectations while producing effective results.

The best candidates for project managers have four areas of competence:

- They are good at thinking — that is, planning, problem solving and information gathering.
- Their self-confidence lets them operate successfully in the uncertain project environment and keeps their tempers even.
- They understand and endorse the business purpose of the project they are managing and can make decisions accordingly.
- They are wonderful with people: motivating, negotiating and dealing with conflict.

The planning team, as project champions, should look for managers skilful in at least three out of four of these areas and at least competent in the fourth.

Project managers may actually do little project work themselves — they are there to *manage*. This means that they balance, and sometimes reprioritise, the three demands of any project — to be as good as possible, given the constraints of time and money available.

How much time to spend

Experience shows that between 5 and 15 per cent of the time planned for a project should be management time; that is, time in addition to the time spent producing deliverables. The average is 10 per cent. For example, a project with a team of ten full-time people should have an eleventh person full time as project manager. By the same arithmetic, one person can manage two five-person teams ... or one five-person team half time and do project work during the other half.

If the project is complex or if it involves many parts of the organisation, it will take more management; if it is simple and the team comes entirely from one department, it may take less. In any case, there should be only one project manager, although some clerical work, such as time reporting, can be delegated.

The ten essentials of project planning

It is the project manager's responsibility to anticipate what has to be done and act accordingly. Successful project planning addresses these ten items:

1. **Clarify goals and objectives**. The initial responsibility of the planning team's project champion is to explain why this project has been launched and its importance to the business.
2. **List all tasks in detail**. Projects miss their deadlines more often because of tasks not planned for than for poor estimates. Include *all* the tasks.
3. **Identify dependencies among tasks**. Some tasks must precede others, and some can be done in parallel with others; use a software package to define and keep track of all the tasks and their dependencies.
4. **Describe the people and resources needed**. Selecting the team and defining special tools, training or facilities follows understanding of the scope and kind of work to be done.
5. **Estimate task times and costs**. Make estimates after the team has been selected; some people work faster than others. The sum of estimated costs is the budget.
6. **Apply a productivity factor**. No one can work full time on a project for all sorts of legitimate reasons: meetings, holidays, training, etc. Expect no more than 75 per cent of

Implementation

a team member's time to be devoted to project work; in some companies this percentage is smaller.

7. **Divide tasks into segments of two weeks or less.** Each segment must have a deliverable that is clearly either done or not done on its due date. A two-week period is about the right balance between overmanaging a task and allowing the assigned person freedom to accomplish the job as they think best. Also, the project will not be more than two weeks behind if the deliverable is late – probably less since at least *some* work will have been done. Remember: with a 75 per cent productivity factor, the 80 calendar hours in two weeks will produce 60 hours of project work.

8. **Establish a change budget.** Padded estimates lead to trouble; reality-based management is best. To the best estimate of project cost, add 10–20 per cent and assign this figure to the budget. An expected rate of change greater than 20 per cent suggests a poorly planned or exceptionally volatile project that probably ought to be reconsidered. Here is an example of budgeting when dealing with a 'customer':

    If the Information Systems Department is building an order processing system for the Sales Department, Sales is the 'customer'. When a change arises from the customer's growing understanding of the features and functions of the project deliverable, from changes in the marketplace, or from some other source, that change must be estimated in terms of its cost to the project in time and money. Then the customer decides whether or not to include the change in the project. If the answer is 'yes', the money for the change is transferred to the project budget which the project manager manages.

9. **Establish a delivery process.** This point is tied closely to item 7. The process of delivering a project's objectives is the delivery of one small element after another to the client. There should be no major surprises and certainly no single large delivery at the end of a long period.

10. **Consider potential problems.** To a remarkable degree, managers can head off or prepare for most of the problems likely to trouble a project, but only if problems are identified. The example below illustrates this.

A solid project plan built by following the ten steps given here ensures project success. Project champions should know that adequate planning saves project time overall. Remember, if the project is even moderately complex — that is, if it has more than about 50 individual tasks — use project management software to establish and control it.

Project Management, in this Better Management Skills series, is full of useful suggestions.

Exercise: Identifying Problems

Follow this example as if you were managing a project to install a custom-made industrial robot:

- Identify each major possible threat to the project; for example, the robot does not arrive on time.
- Name all reasonable causes for this problem: it is not built in time for shipment date, it is not shipped on time or there is a transport breakdown.
- For each cause, determine what can be done to *prevent* its happening; some creativity may be needed here. For this example, consider the 'not built on time' threat. You could stay in touch with the vendor's order processing and production people — perhaps through a customer representative — and you could also offer a bonus for on-time delivery and/or assess a penalty for late delivery.
- For each cause decide how you will know if the problem has occurred or not, and determine how best to protect the project if the problem does occur despite protective measures.

Take the late shipment problem as an example. First of all, staying in touch with the vendor's people is vital. Use what

Implementation

you learn from the vendor's people to assess where their progress actually stands relative to your need for the robot. If you are worried, you might even visit their plant and see if their project manager is planning effectively.

If it looks as though the robot will be late, review your own project progress and decide whether or not the delivery date set when the robot was ordered should be changed. Perhaps the robot is not on the critical path and you have slack time. If so, shift the due date, since this robot is one of a kind.

If the delivery date cannot be shifted, assess the impact of its late arrival on the project and see if you can recover lost days by shortening other tasks on the critical path. Otherwise, share the bad news with the project champion as soon as it is inevitable. Be sure to have options to suggest.

Implementation Worksheet

Before answering the following questions, list the action plans you are going to champion and name the people who will manage them.

_____

_____

_____

1. How much time do these project managers need to manage their projects adequately?

_____

_____

_____

2. If they have other duties, how much time do these take?

_____

_____

_____

3. What is the total number of hours expected of each project manager? Are there any scheduling problems?

_____
_____
_____

4. When will the project managers meet you to go over their project plans?

_____
_____
_____

5. What is a realistic productivity factor for my area of this company?

_____
_____
_____

6. Do the project managers have any shortcomings that may cause complications? How will you address these?

_____
_____
_____

7. Which is the most important consideration in the accomplishment of each project — quality, cost or time spent?

_____
_____
_____

Step 6
Control and Follow-Up

Project control

The planning process behind your company's competitive strategy moves from vision and mission to set goals in key result areas. Action plan projects are initiated to meet those goals. This section tells how to ensure that the benefits promised by those action plans develop on schedule.

The delivery process for each individual action plan project provides basic information for managing the company's planned competitive strategy. As each two-week (or less) task is accomplished, the project has produced one more deliverable — some are more significant than others but all are valuable in the progression. Tracking project progress shows whether or not strategic initiatives are developing on schedule.

The Weekly Project Report form presented here has been designed so that project team members can fill it in quickly and project managers can make rapid summaries. The various items on the form are explained as follows:

- **Accomplishments**
  Each reporting team member uses the task code assigned to every two-week (or less) task to tell what they accomplished and when. Remember, every task was planned with a *done/not done* measure; tasks reported as accomplished have passed the *done* test (specification complete, milling machine hardwired on shop floor, etc). The project manager

uses individual reports to check off completed tasks from the overall project plan. Actual completion dates provide project history and insight into estimating accuracy.
- **Planned tasks**
This is simply a list of what the person reporting plans to do next week. The project manager verifies that these tasks are appropriate in the light of the project schedule.
- **Problems encountered**
Developing new things never progresses smoothly. The project manager needs to know what major problems have been encountered and where they stand. Have they been solved? Should the project manager or champion become involved? Is a pattern emerging?
- **Potential problems**
Project managers are vitally concerned with identifying and heading off potential problems; team members need to extend their project manager's vision by pointing out trouble in time to neutralise it.

Weekly Project Report

Name: *Chris Davies* **Week Ending:** 10/7

Accomplishments
Task ID/Task Name/Date Complete
1874	*Approved bubble wrap specs.*	8/7
1875	*Prep'd wrap purchase order.*	10/7

Planned Tasks for Next Week
Task ID/Task Name/Planned Start Date
1876	*Design outer box*	13/7
1877	*Design 12-pack*	15/7

Problems Encountered
Description/Current Situation
Solving the failure of No 3 wrapping machine took half a day from project; back on track through overtime.

Potential Problems
Description/Prevention/Protection/Information
Bubble Wrap Co in contract negotiations may lead to strike. Can't prevent. Will have alternative supplier ready.

Goals

When complete, some projects produce results immediately (for instance, cutting manufacturing costs by 2 per cent). Others establish initiatives that should become profitable (new product launch, training programmes and so on), but whose value remains to be seen. The results of all projects added together can be compared with key result area goals set during the planning process. These should be evaluated according to the timetable set out during the planning process.

For example, if the *goal* was to increase market share from 12 to 17 per cent, employing the *strategy* of introducing five new products during the next eight months, the *tactics* might have included the following *action plans*:

- **Action plan 1:** Introduce product A by end of first month.
- **Action plan 2:** Introduce product B by end of first six weeks.
- **Action plan 3:** Introduce product C by end of third month.
- **Action plan 4:** Introduce product D by end of sixth month.
- **Action plan 5:** Introduce product E by end of eighth month.

Assuming that each new product will increase market share by 1 per cent eight weeks after introduction, there is a timetable of expected goal achievement that begins two months after product A is introduced and claims an additional 1 per cent market share. Thereafter, products B to E inclusive will be introduced and will mature in the marketplace until – by the end of the tenth month – all five products have market acceptance and the company's market share is up from 12 to 17 per cent.

A similar timetable can be made for every action plan and aggregate of these timetables will forecast expected progress towards company goals over time.

Regular reporting

In the same way that action plan projects need regular weekly reporting, progress towards major corporate goals should be measured regularly. It is a truism of management that what is measured usually improves.

Quarterly meetings of the planning team are the minimum number needed to keep informed of progress towards goals. Probably not everything will go as planned; some initiatives may have to be dropped, others redirected. As action plan champions, the members of the planning team should invite their project managers to present their results and answer questions. It can be a fine learning experience – the planning team will hear the person best qualified to answer questions, and the champions will demonstrate good delegation.

Summary

Planning competitive strategy is not a one-off enterprise. To maintain strategic effectiveness, the management team must meet annually to celebrate progress, analyse problems and modify goals. Typically, they will find themselves enjoying increasingly fruitful discussions as their intelligence gathering grows more and more productive and their ability to think strategically improves. They establish new action plans to succeed the ones completed the year before and formulate ways of sharing good news and bad with the rest of the organisation.

Remember, competitive strategic planning requires practice over time. Experience suggests that a team needs at least three annual sessions to become really proficient. The good news is that team members learn a great deal in the first session, enough to construct a potent competitive strategy; even those who had reservations at first end up looking forward to the next year's session.

Control and Follow-Up Worksheet

1. For the action plan projects you are championing, list their project managers and the dates when they will report progress to you:

   _____

   _____

   _____

   _____

   _____

2. For each action plan for which you are responsible, list the first date each is to have a measurable goal accomplished — and identify what that goal is:

   _____

   _____

   _____

   _____

   _____

3. The competitive strategy planning team will reconvene on this date:

   _____

   _____

   _____

   _____

Better Management Skills

This highly popular range of inexpensive paperbacks covers all areas of basic management. Practical, easy to read and instantly accessible, these guides will help managers to improve their business or communication skills. Those marked * are available on audio cassette.

The books in this series can be tailored to specific company requirements. For further details, please contact the publisher, Kogan Page, telephone 0171 278 0433, fax 0171 837 6348.

Be a Successful Supervisor
Be Positive
Business Etiquette
Business Creativity
Coaching Your Employees
Conducting Effective Interviews
Consulting for Success
Counselling Your Staff
Creative Decision-making
Creative Thinking in Business
Delegating for Results
Effective Employee Participation
Effective Meeting Skills
Effective Performance Appraisals*
Effective Presentation Skills
Empowerment
First Time Supervisor
Get Organised!
Goals and Goal Setting
How to Communicate Effectively*
How to Develop a Positive Attitude*
How to Develop Assertiveness
How to Motivate People*
How to Understand Financial Statements
How to Write a Staff Manual
Improving Employee Performance
Improving Relations at Work

Keeping Customers for Life
Leadership Skills for Women
Learning to Lead
Make Every Minute Count*
Making TQM Work
Managing Cultural Diversity at Work
Managing Disagreement Constructively
Managing Organisational Change
Managing Part-time Employees
Managing Quality Customer Service
Managing Your Boss
Marketing for Success
Memory Skills in Business
Mentoring
Office Management
Personnel Testing
Productive Planning
Project Management
Quality Customer Service
Rate Your Skills as a Manager
Sales Training Basics
Self-Managing Teams
Selling Professionally
Successful Negotiation
Successful Presentation Skills
Successful Telephone Techniques
Systematic Problem-solving and Decision-making
Team Building
Training Methods that Work
The Woman Manager